HORSE & PONY
SHOWS
&EVENTS

HORSE & PONY
SHOWS
&EVENTS

Carolyn Henderson

Foreword by Carl Hester

DORLING KINDERSLEY
London • New York • Sydney • Moscow
www.dk.com

A DORLING KINDERSLEY BOOK
www.dk.com

Project Editor Maggie Crowley
Project Art Editor Sharon Grant
Editor Kathleen Bada
Designer Darren Holt
Managing Editor Jayne Parsons
Managing Art Editor Gill Shaw

DTP Designer Nomazwe Madonko
Picture Researcher Francis Vargo
Jacket Design Margherita Gianni
Production Lisa Moss
Photography Andy Crawford and John Henderson

First published in Great Britain in 1999 by
Dorling Kindersley Limited
9 Henrietta Street, London WC2E 8PS

2 4 6 8 10 9 7 5 3 1

Copyright © 1999 Dorling Kindersley Limited, London

A CIP catalogue record for this book is available from the British Library.

ISBN 0 7513 5946 7

Colour reproduction by Colourscan, Singapore

Printed and bound in Italy by L.E.G.O.

CONTENTS

FOREWORD

COMPETING IS FUN and exciting. It tests all your riding, schooling, and horse care skills – and whether or not you come home with a rosette, it will help you build a winning partnership with your horse. Successful competing depends on the right preparations, whether you are riding at international level, like me, or starting out. This book will tell you all you need to know when you are riding or watching others. It will help you choose the right sport, get your horse fit, and school it so you are confident and safe. Enjoy your reading – and your riding!

CRHester

CARL HESTER,
INTERNATIONAL DRESSAGE RIDER

WHAT TO ENTER

WHATEVER SORT OF riding you enjoy, you can also compete. There are competitions at all levels to suit everyone from the beginner to the advanced rider, and from the novice horse to the experienced one. Everyone likes to win prizes, but competing is more than that. It allows you to monitor your progress and that of your horse, and have fun at the same time.

Horse and rider in harmony

Half pass is an advanced dressage movement.

Dressage

Dressage demonstrates the horse's balance and suppleness, the rider's skill, and the communication between horse and rider. Riders perform tests made up of a series of movements, which are judged for accuracy and harmony.

Rider in forward position and in balance with horse

Fly fringes are permitted in the showjumping ring for protection against flies.

Showjumping

Show-jumpers need to be balanced and athletic. Their riders' aim is to complete a course of fences without penalties for knockdowns or refusals, often against the clock. Puissance competitions have fewer fences and test how high a horse can jump. All horses and ponies can be taught to jump, but some have more natural talent for it than others.

Endurance

This is a fast-growing sport. There are local and international competitions that range from about 32 km (20 miles) to more than 160 km (100 miles). Many riders also take part in non-competitive pleasure rides of 16–24 km (10–15 miles).

Eventing

Horse trials, or eventing, is the ultimate challenge. There are three phases – dressage, showjumping, and cross-country. Top-level three-day events include steeplechase, and roads and tracks phases. Horses must be calm and obedient for dressage, bold for cross-country, and balanced and careful for showjumping.

Showing

Showing classes are judged on a horse's or pony's conformation, movement, and ride. A good show horse or pony must be well-schooled with good manners. Different countries have different types of show class. Equitation classes focus purely on the rider – the horse is not judged.

Top hats are only worn for formal occasions.

Black jacket adds to elegance.

GETTING FIT TO COMPETE

COMPETING IS HARD WORK, so you and your horse need to be fit. A programme of gradually increasing work will develop your horse's strength, suppleness, and stamina. Check that your horse is healthy before you start and that its teeth and feet are in good shape. Ask advice on what, and how much, to feed your horse. Cycling and swimming are ways to increase your fitness.

Getting your horse fit

Getting a horse fit requires different types of work. Hacking, starting with short periods of walk, then increasing to longer, faster rides, builds a horse's stamina and overall fitness. Schooling makes it more supple and helps build up muscle, while gymnastic jumping, or gridwork, makes it more athletic.

Rider works on transitions between paces and large turns to increase horse's suppleness.

A schooled horse should work on the bit when it has warmed up, so that it is well balanced and responsive to the rider's aids.

Horse should have active paces.

WE

1 –

3 –

5 –

7 –

HELP FROM OTHERS
If you have little time to ride your pony, knowledgeable parents or friends may be able to help. Correct lungeing is useful for ponies who are too small for adults; make sure your pony is not lunged more than three times a week, or it will get bored. When lungeing, work on both reins and increase the amount of work from 10 to 20 minutes.

Wear gloves when lungeing.

Side reins encourage pony to accept the bit.

EXERCISE ROUTINE

It is important to keep an exercise routine so you can judge the progress of your horse and spot potential problems. You must feed correctly; balance forage (grass and hay) with hard feed (mix or nuts). Increase feed gradually; give more forage than hard feed.

ROADWORK	SCHOOLING & GRIDWORK	HACKING	FEED	CHECKLIST
Walk your horse on level ground for up to 20 minutes a day, building up to 45 minutes. Avoid any hill work.	*Walk should be active and balanced.*	Feed a horse on a ratio of 75–100% forage to 0–75% hard feed, such as nuts and horse mix.		If your horse is very unfit, extend the amount of walking exercise up to about six weeks.
Introduce short periods of working, rising trot. Do not work at sitting trot. Increase rides out by up to one hour.	Start to school for 15–20 minutes, twice a week. Practise different exercises, such as large circles. Introduce canter in week four.	Hack out four to five days a week. Introduce gradual hill work. Always walk downhill, but ride at a balanced trot uphill.	If in regular work, increase ratio of hard feed to 50%. *A scoop of mix*	Increase the amount of exercise a horse has before increasing its feed, not vice versa. Continue to turn your horse out daily to help it relax.
Basic work to strengthen tendons and ligaments now complete. Horse should have reached basic level of fitness.	School at walk, trot, and canter three times a week, with short hacks if necessary.	When not schooling, take longer hacks up to one-and-a-half hours. Ride up steep hills if possible.	If necessary, increase feed in line with horse's work.	Check horse's legs daily for signs of injury or lameness. Forage should not be less than 50% of diet for ponies and most horses.
Trotting poles help to improve balance.	Introduce gridwork as part of two schooling sessions a week. Gradually build up the heights and numbers of fences.	Continue with longer hacks, including steep hills. Start fast work, but on ground that will not jar horse's hooves.	Increase feed to peak level, but continue to monitor horse's condition and reduce hard feed if horse is fit enough.	Check fit of saddle. A horse that builds up muscle through schooling will continue to change shape.

CLOTHES AND TACK

CLOTHES AND TACK must be safe, comfortabl and suitable for the horse and rider, and the type of event they are entering. It is best to get expert advice on fitting tack, and to use equipment such as helmets and body protectors that meet the latest safety standards. Using damaged equipment increases the risk of accidents.

Safety helmet with chin-strap

Hacking jacket with shirt and tie

Beige jodhpurs

Full-length leather boots

WHAT TO WEAR
This rider is dressed smartly for general riding in competition. She could enter basic dressage, showing, and showjumping classes. Higher-level competition may require more formal clothes.

Special equipment
Different types of competitions require special equipment. Dressage, showjumping, horse trials, and Western classes all have rules about what the rider and horse should wear.

Safety helmets with coloured silks are worn for eventing and long-distance riding.

Body protector helps prevent serious injury in the event of a fall.

Flash noseband prevents horse from opening its mouth, giving rider greater control.

Brushing boots protect the horse on front and hind legs.

CROSS-COUNTRY CLOTHES
Jumping at speed means that horse and rider need protective equipment. A rider may use different or additional tack, such as a breastplate for control.

Over-reach boots

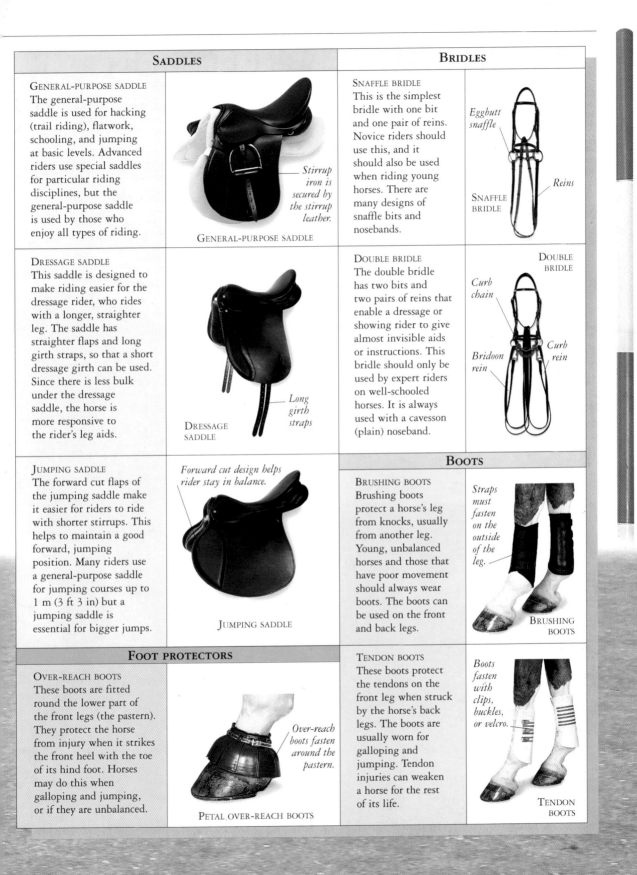

SADDLES	BRIDLES

GENERAL-PURPOSE SADDLE

The general-purpose saddle is used for hacking (trail riding), flatwork, schooling, and jumping at basic levels. Advanced riders use special saddles for particular riding disciplines, but the general-purpose saddle is used by those who enjoy all types of riding.

Stirrup iron is secured by the stirrup leather.

GENERAL-PURPOSE SADDLE

SNAFFLE BRIDLE

This is the simplest bridle with one bit and one pair of reins. Novice riders should use this, and it should also be used when riding young horses. There are many designs of snaffle bits and nosebands.

Eggbutt snaffle

Reins

SNAFFLE BRIDLE

DRESSAGE SADDLE

This saddle is designed to make riding easier for the dressage rider, who rides with a longer, straighter leg. The saddle has straighter flaps and long girth straps, so that a short dressage girth can be used. Since there is less bulk under the dressage saddle, the horse is more responsive to the rider's leg aids.

Long girth straps

DRESSAGE SADDLE

DOUBLE BRIDLE

The double bridle has two bits and two pairs of reins that enable a dressage or showing rider to give almost invisible aids or instructions. This bridle should only be used by expert riders on well-schooled horses. It is always used with a cavesson (plain) noseband.

DOUBLE BRIDLE

Curb chain

Bridoon rein

Curb rein

JUMPING SADDLE

The forward cut flaps of the jumping saddle make it easier for riders to ride with shorter stirrups. This helps to maintain a good forward, jumping position. Many riders use a general-purpose saddle for jumping courses up to 1 m (3 ft 3 in) but a jumping saddle is essential for bigger jumps.

Forward cut design helps rider stay in balance.

JUMPING SADDLE

BOOTS

BRUSHING BOOTS

Brushing boots protect a horse's leg from knocks, usually from another leg. Young, unbalanced horses and those that have poor movement should always wear boots. The boots can be used on the front and back legs.

Straps must fasten on the outside of the leg.

BRUSHING BOOTS

FOOT PROTECTORS

OVER-REACH BOOTS

These boots are fitted round the lower part of the front legs (the pastern). They protect the horse from injury when it strikes the front heel with the toe of its hind foot. Horses may do this when galloping and jumping, or if they are unbalanced.

Over-reach boots fasten around the pastern.

PETAL OVER-REACH BOOTS

TENDON BOOTS

These boots protect the tendons on the front leg when struck by the horse's back legs. The boots are usually worn for galloping and jumping. Tendon injuries can weaken a horse for the rest of its life.

Boots fasten with clips, buckles, or velcro.

TENDON BOOTS

GROOMED TO PERFECTION

SPECIAL GROOMING and plaiting techniques make a horse look its best for competitions. A clean, shiny coat is essential, and plaiting and quarter marks show off good conformation. Some breeds, such as Arabs and mountain and moorland ponies, should not be shown with plaited manes or tails.

QUARTER MARKS
Quarter marks show off the hindquarters. To make them, dampen the hair and make squares or diamonds by combing down against the lay of the hair. Alternatively, use a plastic template.

Quarter marks

Plaiting the tail
Many people prefer plaited tails to pulled ones, which have long side hairs pulled out. You can only plait a full tail. Take in just a few hairs at a time and keep your plait tight as you work down the tail.

1 Dividing the hairs
Take small sections of hair from each side at the top of the tail. Cross the sections over and take a third from one side of the tail and bring it to the centre.

Start right at the top and keep sections tight for neatness.

Pass side sections over the centre.

Keep hold of the centre plait ends so that the whole plait remains tight.

2 Plait down the tail
Bring in small sections from each side and join them with the central plait. Plait down until the centre plait reaches two thirds of the way down the dock.

3 Loop plait under tail
Continue plaiting without joining new hair. Loop the end under and stitch in place.

White socks and markings should be spotless.

Plaiting the mane

A plaited mane shows off a horse's neck. Pull or shorten the mane to about 5 in (12 cms) long before plaiting, and thin it if necessary. Although rubber bands are quick to use, plaits sewn with thread look smarter and stay in place longer.

1 Divide mane into bunches
First dampen mane with water or hair gel. Then divide the mane into as many equal bunches as suits the length of the horse's neck. Fasten each bunch with a rubber band.

2 Plait down mane
Plait each bunch, keeping the plait tight so that short hairs stay in place. Double up the end hairs and fasten with a band or plaiting thread that is the same colour as the horse's mane.

3 Roll up plait on crest
If using thread, pass needle through top of plait. Roll plait up to the crest. Stitch the plaits in place, or fasten them with rubber bands.

Some people use petroleum jelly for shine around eyes and mouth.

Whiskers may be trimmed for neatness.

Set plaits on top of a thin neck and to the side of a heavy one.

A WELL-GROOMED HORSE
Daily grooming helps to maintain healthy skin and a shiny coat. Grease and dust dull the hair. If the weather is warm, you may want to bath your horse before a competition. A little coat gloss applied with a soft cloth adds extra shine for special occasions.

Take extra care when washing the tail of an inexperienced horse.

Hoof oil or polish should be used only for shows. Ask your farrier for advice on keeping hooves healthy.

Fetlock hair and hair around coronet neatly trimmed.

Washing the tail

To wash a tail, stand to one side of the horse. Wet the hair, then work in a horse shampoo. Massage the top of the tail with your fingers to loosen grease or dirt, then work down the length of the tail. Rinse thoroughly and repeat if necessary. Squeeze out the water, then dry the tail by gently swishing it in circles.

15

PREPARING FOR A SHOW

START SHOW PREPARATION early; make sure your horse is fit and that your tack and equipment are in good condition. Your horse must be well shod and its vaccinations, or any other documents, must be up to date. Plan ahead and check when your class starts, then work out when you need to arrive at the show.

Pre-show preparation
Prepare as much as possible the day before a show. Clean your tack, make sure your clothes are clean, and, if necessary, bath your horse. You may want to plait your horse the day before if you have a very early start. Make a list of things you need to take and get them ready in advance.

Hard hat and gloves

Black or blue show jacket

Stock with tie pin

Long boots are usually worn by older riders. Younger riders normally wear jodhpur boots.

SHOWING CLOTHES
For a showing class or dressage wear a hard hat and gloves, and either a black or blue jacket with stock and stockpin, or a tweed jacket with shirt and tie. Choose beige breeches and long black boots or short jodhpur boots.

Travel boots for horse

Bridle

Breastplate stops saddle from slipping

Long-sleeved shirt for cross-country events

Overgirth worn over saddle in cross-country events

Saddle with girth, stirrups, and leathers

Filled haynet

Water container

First-aid kit for horse

Water bucket

Tail guard to protect tail while travelling

Mobile phone in case of emergency

Studs for shoes

Over-reach boots

First-aid kit for rider

Grease – use on horse's legs to help it slide over fences

Brushing boots

Grooming kit

Cooler rug

Feed, if needed

Long riding boots

Getting to the show

Allow plenty of time to load your horse and drive to the show. Make sure your horse wears protective travelling gear and a suitable rug. Check that you have packed all the things you need for the day before loading your horse.

Ramps should have non-slip surfaces and must be stable and level, to give the horse confidence as it walks up.

Look ahead and calmly lead horse up the ramp.

Leg guards protect horse's legs while travelling.

Allow extra time for a young or inexperienced horse to settle when you arrive at the show.

Cover up your show clothes or change into them later.

THE HORSE BOX
Vehicles must be light and inviting so the horse can see where it is going when loading. There must be enough headroom and each section inside the box must be wide enough for the size of horse.

Arrival

Try and arrive at the showground an hour before your class starts. Check that your horse has not sweated up or injured itself on the way to the show. Find out if classes are running on time, collect numbers and make entries if necessary. Tack up and walk round until your horse settles, then warm up without tiring it out.

Stand to one side in case your horse kicks out in excitement.

BEFORE SHOW

- Check horse is shod and its vaccinations are up to date

- Check clothes and tack are clean and in good condition

- If you have an early start, bath and plait horse day before show

- Check time of your class so that you can arrange to arrive at show on time

YOUR FIRST SHOW

YOUR FIRST SHOW is likely to be a small, local competition with classes for novice horses and riders. These classes may include clear round jumping, equitation classes, and competitions for best turned out horse and rider. Shows with dressage tests at beginner level are also suitable. Do not enter more than two classes or your horse may become tired, especially if it is inexperienced.

If your horse is inexperienced you may just want to watch for the first time.

THE COLLECTING RING
Go to the collecting ring before your class starts, as you may need to register your show number with an official. Check how many competitors there are before your turn, so that you allow yourself time to warm up. Look out for other riders in the collecting ring, especially near practice jumps. Be ready to enter the show ring when called.

What to expect
At a show, you will see lots of horses, people, and vehicles, and you may hear loud-speaker announcements. Classes are held in areas called rings, and areas where people warm up are called collecting rings. Show officials will give you a number to wear and they will tell you when it is your turn to compete.

If riding near parked horseboxes, watch out for other horses being unloaded.

Clear round jumping

Clear round jumping is a good introduction to showjumping for inexperienced horses and riders. You pay a small fee each time you attempt the course, and if you have problems, such as a refusal, you can try again. There is no jump-off, but usually each rider who jumps a clear round gets a special rosette. Think of it as a schooling round, not as a competition.

Rider looks ahead to next jump.

Clear round jumps are low, usually between 1 ft 6 in (45 cm) and 2 ft 6 in (75 cm). The jumps usually include small fillers and easy doubles.

ENJOYING YOUR SHOW

Shows should be fun for you and your horse. You may feel nervous at first, but concentrate on riding and caring for your horse correctly and you will soon feel more confident.

If something goes wrong, try not to panic. Keep calm, and remember that you will always have another chance, and that you and your horse will improve with practise.

	BEFORE THE SHOW	AT THE SHOW	IN THE RING	AFTER THE SHOW
PONY WELL-BEING	Allow plenty of time to load your horse into the horse box and to get to the show, so that both you and your horse are calm on arrival.	Do not ride your horse all day; get off and offer it water often. If your horse needs a feed, allow an hour for digestion before riding.	Stay calm if things go wrong. Do not panic or lose your temper – practising at home will help you avoid problems next time.	Check that there are no minor injuries or loose shoes. Once back at home, your horse should be calm and comfortable, and not sweating.
HORSE AND RIDER SAFETY	Check that your tack, clothes, and other equipment are clean and in good repair. Horse's shoes must be secure and in good condition.	Beware of excitable horses – do not ride within kicking distance of other horses. Do not ride on pedestrian-only walkways.	Walk calmly into and out of the ring.	Clean tack, clothes, and any other equipment. Check all tack for breakages and send off for repair if necessary.
RIDER MANNERS (ETIQUETTE)	Thank those who have helped you get ready for the show, such as friends and the horsebox driver. They will be happy to help you again.	Check in with ring official ten minutes before your turn. Ride in collecting ring for your class and do not monopolize the practice fence.	Be courteous to other riders. Observe instructions given by officials. Acknowledge and thank judges where appropriate.	Do not criticise judges' decisions. Avoid temptation to leave muck from horsebox at showground. Take all litter home.

GYMKHANAS

GYMKHANAS, or mounted games, are fast and fun. The word gymkhana originates from India; it means a meeting place for equestrian sports. Ponies are better at gymkhana games than horses because they are smaller and easier to turn and to vault on to. Riders have to be as quick and athletic as their ponies.

Mounted games

Balance and co-ordination are vital when taking part in mounted games. They can be played in teams or as individuals, and include bending races, in which riders have to ride in and out of a line of poles without touching any, and flag races, in which riders place flags in containers while on galloping ponies.

Tent pegging

Tent pegging is a military sport that began in India. An individual, or a team of four riders, carries a 3-m (10-ft) lance and gallops towards a row of tent pegs in the ground. The aim is to push the lance through the ring on the peg and lift it out without slowing down.

Fellow rider holds the pony with its reins in place, ready for the rider to vault on.

Speed and schooling

A good gymkhana pony has to be as well-schooled as a top polo pony. It must learn to twist and turn as the rider's bodyweight shifts, and to turn at speed. It is important that you do not pull on the pony's mouth, so try to teach the pony to neck rein, so that it turns from the pressure of the reins against its neck, not pressure on its mouth.

Agility and obedience is important for mounted games. The pony needs to turn tightly round cones, while the rider needs to be equally agile to stay in balance and save time.

The flag race is the gymkhana version of tent pegging.

Long sleeves protect rider's arms from scrapes in case of fall.

Vaulting

Mounting a moving pony is an essential skill for gymkhanas. To vault on, run alongside the pony for a couple of strides and use the momentum of its movement to help push you off the ground as you jump. Swing your right leg well clear of the pony's hindquarters and land in the saddle as lightly as possible.

To vault, practise running alongside your pony with the stirrups flapping. Keep feet clear of irons until mounted.

This pony wears protective tendon and over-reach boots.

SHOWING

WHATEVER TYPE OF horse or pony you ride, you can enjoy showing. There are classes for different breeds, types, and even colours. Some classes are judged on the horse's conformation, movement, and performance in the ring; others assess the rider's ability. There are also in-hand classes, in which the horse is led rather than ridden. Horses must always be beautifully turned out.

Showing side-saddle

Side-saddle classes are judged on either the rider's ability or the horse's conformation and suitability to be ridden side-saddle. The rider's outfit is called a habit, which consists of a jacket and an apron worn over breeches and boots.

Rider must sit straight and look ahead, not tilt to one side.

Ridden classes

Show horses must be schooled and well-behaved. In some classes you will be asked to give an individual show in front of the judge. This means riding your horse to show that it is obedient in all its paces. Sometimes the judge will ride each horse before deciding on final placings. You may be asked to trot your horse in-hand to show off its movement.

The judge may ask you to ride particular exercises, such as a figure of eight.

Standing in a line-up takes practice. Your horse must be able to stand quietly and to walk away from others when asked.

Riders should wear a black, blue, or tweed jacket.

In-hand showing

There are classes for all types of horses and ponies, including young ones, and for different types and breeds. The judge assesses a horse's conformation, so you and your horse must be able to stand still, as well as walk and trot willingly without pulling or hanging back. Your horse must also be well-behaved with others.

The handler should look smart and be able to control a horse. A hat, jacket, shirt and tie, and beige trousers should be worn.

Walk and trot your horse straight towards the judge to show how it moves.

The judge will ask riders to perform some exercises.

Riding without stirrups shows the rider's balance.

Equitation classes

If you cannot find a suitable showing class for your horse, you can have fun in equitation classes. These are judged on the rider's ability, not on the horse's looks. You will be asked to ride different exercises, such as figures of eight and riding without stirrups. Competitors may be asked to ride each other's ponies as well as their own.

SHOWING

• The pony and its tack must be spotlessly clean

• Find out if your horse should be shown with a plaited mane. Some breeds, such as mountain and moorland ponies, are not plaited

• Measure your horse, as some classes specify maximum heights for horses and ponies

• Good manners and schooling are as important as good conformation

DRESSAGE

THERE ARE DRESSAGE TESTS for horses and riders at all stages of training. Tests comprise a series of movements designed to show that the horse is obedient and that the rider uses the correct aids. Beginner level tests include simple movements, such as circles.

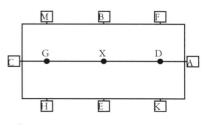

DRESSAGE ARENA
Tests for beginners are ridden in an arena measuring 40 x 20 m (130 x 66 ft). Letters around the arena indicate where a rider should start different dressage movements.

DRESSAGE MOVEMENTS

20-METRE CIRCLE
Dressage tests for beginners include the 20-metre circle, which is ridden in trot or canter. The circle can start from A, C, B, or E. Marks are deducted if the circles are squashed or egg-shaped, so ride in a true circle.

20-METRE CIRCLE

DOWN CENTRE LINE
Tests always start and finish by riding down the centre line. Be positive as you ride down the line and look where you are going, so that you are able to guide your horse in a straight line.

DOWN CENTRE LINE

SERPENTINE LOOPS
A three-loop serpentine is one of the most difficult movements in beginner tests. The loops must be equal in size and the rider should ride straight across the centre line before starting another loop.

SERPENTINE LOOPS

SHALLOW LOOPS
Loops of 3 m (10 ft) or 5 m (16 ft) are ridden down the long side of the arena, between the two outside markers, H and K, or F and M. While riding the loop, horse and rider should maintain a steady rhythm.

SHALLOW LOOPS

Turnout

A dressage rider and horse should be clean, tidy, and neat. At beginner level, riders wear either a tweed jacket with a shirt and tie, or a black jacket and stock. Jodhpurs can be beige or white, and boots can be long or short.

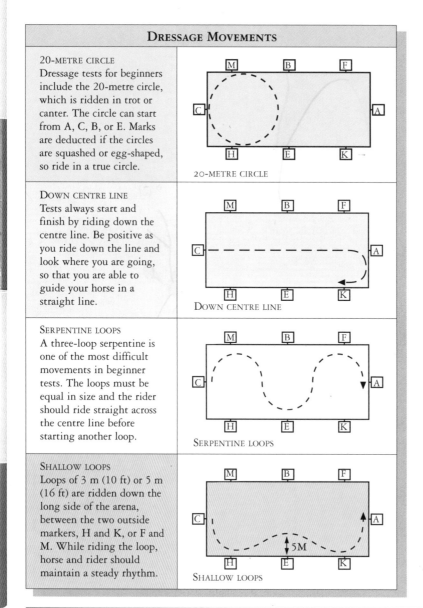

Tails can be pulled or plaited. Pulled tails need bandaging to keep them in shape.

Collected paces

At advanced levels of dressage, horse and rider are asked to work in collected paces. When a horse is collected, it is similar to a coiled spring, full of controlled energy. The horse's steps are shorter and higher than in other paces and its hindlegs come farther under its body. The rider sits tall and light in the saddle to present an elegant picture.

Rider creates energy using leg aids, but controls the pace using weight and hands, without pulling back.

A plaited mane looks smart and helps create a good impression.

CORRECT EQUIPMENT
Riders can carry whips and wear spurs in dressage tests but must not misuse them. Martingales are not allowed but neckstraps, breastplates, and breastgirths are. Only certain bits and nosebands are allowed.

Snaffle bridles are used at beginner level.

Rider's legs create energy to lengthen stride without increasing speed.

Dressage riders should check a dressage rule book to make sure clothes and tack comply with their level of competition. Using wrong tack will result in elimination.

Hooves are oiled for competition.

Extended paces

In extended paces, the horse's stride should be as long as possible. It is important that the horse stays balanced and does not pull or lean on the rider's hands. Beginner level tests ask for lengthened strides, which are easier to perform. This is the first step to producing the extended paces of the advanced horse.

DRESSAGE TESTS

A DRESSAGE TEST is a series of movements performed in front of judges to show that a horse is obedient and supple, and that a rider's position and use of aids are correct. Each movement in a dressage test carries up to ten marks. At the end of the competition, the judge gives the riders a sheet with marks and comments about their test. These help riders decide what they need to practise before their next competition.

Rider practises different movements.

LEARNING YOUR TEST
Some people learn tests by drawing diagrams of the movements in the correct order; others walk the test on foot. Practise the movements with your horse, but ride them in a different order. Do not ride the complete test too many times or your horse may start to anticipate what comes next.

Top level horses often have plaits fastened with white tape.

Dressage riders plan time to warm up, making sure the horse is not too fresh or too tired when it starts the test.

Concentrate on keeping the horse balanced and energetic before entering the arena.

Bandages used for warming up must be removed before starting the test.

Make sure you know the positions of the letters.

Practise movements that you and your horse are good at. If you attempt movements that you find difficult, your horse may become tense. Concentrate on building its energy and responsiveness.

Warming up

There will probably be a special area or school for warming up at the show. Other riders will also be using the practice area so be aware of where they are going. Start your warming up on a loose rein so your horse stretches its muscles. You may need up to half an hour to warm up. Try to stay relaxed, so that you do not make your horse tense.

Riding the test

As you enter the arena, look up and smile. Try to keep your breathing steady to help you stay calm. Make sure your horse is moving energetically so you ride a straight line down the centre without leaving the centre line. If you make a mistake, keep calm – you will have lost marks for only one movement. Remember to smile and salute the judge at the end of your test.

Dressage judges look for a horse and rider that make an elegant picture together. Movements must be accurate and performed at the right place.

Advanced horses, such as this, wear double bridles. Beginner level horses always wear snaffle bridles.

Rider's hands are sensitive and do not pull on the reins.

SHOWJUMPING

THERE ARE SHOWJUMPING competitions for ponies and horses at all levels, ranging from small local shows to international competitions. The aim of riding a course is always to have a clear round without knocking down any fences. A course is often ridden against the clock, and the fastest clear round wins. Top level Puissance competitions test the horse's ability to jump great heights, often 2 m (6 ft 6 in) or more.

A body protector should be worn, even when practising.

Brushing boots protect the horse's legs when it is jumping.

Novice classes

Novice classes are for inexperienced horses or riders. Fences should be low and there should be no difficult turns or tricky distances between jumps. Clear round classes, in which the aim is to jump a clear round, are an ideal introduction to showjumping. Many shows allow you to attempt more than one round so that you gain extra experience.

Distances between jumps for showjumping courses are based on a horse's canter stride measuring 3.7 m (12 ft). Ask advice when measuring distances for a pony.

SEEING A STRIDE
Learning to ride a balanced, rhythmic canter can help you meet the take-off point for a fence correctly. This is called "seeing a stride." A good way to learn how to do this is to lay a course of poles on the ground and practise riding over them in a flowing rhythm.

Rider looks ahead to the next jump.

Gridwork

Gridwork helps you and your horse to become confident and athletic. A grid is a row of fences spaced at the correct distance for a horse's stride. This makes it easier for the horse to find the correct take-off points. The distances are shorter for ponies than for horses. Get an expert to help set up the grid, and always have someone on the ground who can alter the distances if necessary.

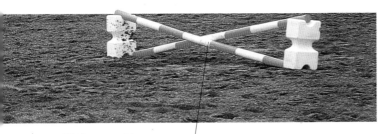

Riding a grid encourages you to improve your rhythm and to ride in a straight line.

Types of jump

Fences can be uprights or spreads, and a course will have both. Courses will include rustic poles, planks, coloured fillers, brush fences, walls, and gates. Advanced courses may have water jumps. Your instructor will help you introduce your horse to different types of fence so that you and your horse approach a jump confidently.

Poles are placed at set distances on the ground.

A spread fence encourages a horse to take off correctly and jump in style.

DISTANCES BETWEEN JUMPS
Distances between fences are set to allow a certain number of strides between them. At advanced level you may need to shorten or lengthen your horse's stride to meet a fence correctly.

A double, two fences set at a distance, allows one or two non-jumping strides between a fence.

Fillers test horse's and rider's confidence and concentration. Some horses may shy away from fillers.

IN THE RING

WHEN YOU FIRST START jumping at competitions, choose courses that have slightly smaller fences than you jump at home. This gives you and your horse confidence when jumping in strange surroundings. Walk the course carefully, and allow time to warm up before you enter the ring. If you jump a clear round and have a long wait before a jump-off, ride over two or three practice fences just before your turn.

WALKING THE COURSE
A rider can see potential challenges in the ring, such as fences on slightly uphill or downhill approaches, by walking the course. Walk the track you intend to ride so you know which route to take once you are on the horse. In novice classes, distances between combination fences are usually straightforward, but in higher level competitions distances are more complicated.

Once your horse is jumping happily, stop. Do not tire a horse before it goes into the jumping ring.

A helper adjusts the practice fence, by gradually making it taller until it is competition height.

Warming up

Allow about half an hour to warm up before you enter the show ring. First try to make your horse obedient and attentive, then establish a rhythmic canter. Next, jump a few upright and spread practice fences. Practice fences should be no higher than the course you are competing over. Be considerate to other riders in the practice ring.

Do not jump a practice fence too many times; six to ten turns is usually enough.

Riding the course

Enter the jumping ring calmly and set up a balanced canter until you receive the signal to start. Approach the first fence calmly but positively. Always look up and ahead to the next fence; never look back if you hit one, as this will unbalance your horse. As you change direction for each jump, make sure your horse is on the correct leg for canter; come back to trot if necessary. Finally, jump fences straight on, not at an angle.

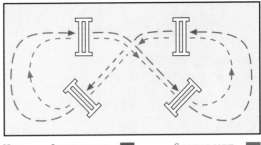

KEY   LONG ROUTE ■   SHORT ROUTE ■

JUMP-OFF

Most jumping classes have a timed jump-off for all riders who go clear in the first round. At home, practise taking a shorter route without spoiling your horse's approach or balance. Making good turns saves more time than galloping between fences, and you will be less likely to hit poles.

Rider is looking up and ahead to next jump.

Rider is keeping light rein contact that does not restrict horse.

Rider is in perfect balance. She has folded forward from the hips, and her weight is absorbed through her knee and ankle joints.

CROSS-COUNTRY

JUMPING CROSS-COUNTRY fences requires courage from both horse and rider. Fences cannot be knocked down, and are tackled at a faster speed than showjumps. If the rider and horse wear correct protective equipment, and if the horse is well-schooled, riding cross-country can be safe and fun. Cross-country jumping can be a competition in its own right or part of a horse trial, in which riders also take part in dressage and showjumping.

Jumping technique

To be successful at riding cross-country, a rider must be able to ride at speed, while in control. The rider should maintain a rhythm with the horse's stride so that it meets fences without having to speed up and slow down each time. The rider must keep in balance with the horse even when things go wrong.

Crash helmets and body protectors must be worn to minimize injury if the rider falls.

The red flag must always be on the right as you jump the fence.

Difficult fences

Some cross-country fences are difficult and need careful riding. To tackle a water jump a horse needs power, not speed, so it does not stumble. Drop fences should be approached with energy and impulsion, but more slowly than ordinary fences. To jump a bounce fence, the rider must be balanced, so that the horse lands over one fence and immediately takes off over another without taking a stride.

JUMPING INTO DARKNESS

Jumping into darkness, perhaps from a field into woods, is difficult for a horse. The rider should approach the fence in a straight line, so that the horse can adjust its eyesight to the changing conditions. By sitting up and riding with determination, the rider can control the horse's pace.

Landing in water slows the horse down, so a controlled approach is vital.

QUICK ROUTES

On a cross-country course, there is often a choice of routes over single fences, and over combinations with more than one jump. The quicker routes are usually more difficult, and are only suitable for experienced horses and riders. If riders are unsure, they take the slower route.

Eventing

Eventing, or horse trials, is the most challenging of all equestrian sports. Riders have to perform a dressage test, then ride a cross-country course and a round of showjumps. Novice events are run over one day, and intermediate and advanced competitions take place over two and three days. Two- and three-day events include speed and endurance sections over a short course of steeplechase fences, and roads and tracks.

Breastgirth or breastplate helps prevent saddle slipping back.

Grease on horse's legs helps it slide over fences, thus preventing serious injury.

ENDURANCE RIDING

Rider and horse must be fit.

COMPETITIVE ENDURANCE rides range from 40 km (25 miles) to more than 160 km (100 miles). There are also non-competitive pleasure rides of about 16 km (10 miles). Arabs and part-bred Arabs are the most popular types of endurance horse at top-level, but any fit horse or pony should manage shorter distances.

Long-distance riding

Long-distance rides must be completed at set speeds, so riders have to judge the speed of their horses' trot and canter. Riders also monitor their horses' heart and breathing rates to make sure they pass the vet checks along the way.

Support team ensures that horse does not catch a chill.

SUPPORT TEAM
The support team, called the crew, is vital at top-level competitive endurance riding. Each rider has a crew to meet up with at various points on a long ride. The crew cools down the horse and makes sure it is comfortable; it also provides the horse with food and water when necessary.

Sloshing down is the safest way to cool down a hot horse. Members of the support team pour water over the horse and walk it round.

Endurance horses are usually allowed to eat and drink small amounts along the ride to help maintain their energy levels.

A fit horse should not get muscle cramps.

The vet will not allow a lame or sick horse to continue.

VETERINARY CHECKS
Veterinary surgeons check horses at "vet gates" – marked stages along the ride. The vets check that heart and breathing rates are correct and that the horse is not lame or injured. A horse that is breathing too fast is not allowed to continue until it has settled.

Horse trails

Organized rides lasting half a day or more are called treks or trail rides. Riders can take their own horse, if it is fit enough, or they can join an organized holiday. Horses need to be sure-footed and sensible, especially on moorland or in mountainous areas. Riders who enjoy this sort of riding may go on to take part in competitive rides.

PLEASURE RIDES
Pleasure and sponsored rides are organized rides that follow a set route; some include optional jumps. These types of rides are not competitions, but riders may be asked to raise sponsorship for a charity. Pleasure rides are a good introduction to long-distance riding for young horses, since they learn to behave in unusual surroundings.

Bred for endurance

An endurance horse must have strong legs and feet, so that it can cope with long rides. The Arab has always been a popular breed with endurance riders. It has natural stamina, speed, and agility. Although lightly built, it can carry weight. Anglo-Arabs, part-bred Arabs, and Standardbreds are also popular.

An Arab has natural balance to cope with difficult terrain.

Horses must be agile to cope with mountainous terrain.

RACING SPORTS

The Kentucky Derby is run on a "dirt track". This all-weather surface does not freeze.

MANY RACING SPORTS are for Thoroughbreds, but there are also specialist races for Quarter horses, Arabs, and harness horses. Top racehorses are among the most valuable in the world; winners of the world's most prestigious races can be worth millions. Ridden horses can be raced on the flat or over jumps. To train riding or driving horses to achieve racing speeds requires special skill and courage.

Flat racing

Some racehorses are bred to run on the flat. They are backed as yearlings and raced as two- and three-year-olds, but often retire at an early age. Flat racehorses are handicapped by weight according to their age and past performance; this makes races more competitive. Prestigious races include the Kentucky Derby, the English Derby, and the Prix de l'Arc de Triomphe in France.

Riders that race on horseback are called jockeys.

Jockeys wear crash helmets covered with coloured silks.

Steeplechasing

Thoroughbred steeplechasers start their racing careers when they are about four years old. The sport started in Ireland, when two riders raced between the steeples of two churches. Today the sport is most popular in the British Isles, but also takes place on a small scale in the US and Europe. Famous races include the Grand National in the UK and the Pardubice in the Czech Republic.

Steeplechasers jump high, fixed fences at racing speeds over distances of up to 7 km (4.5 miles).

Harness racing

Harness racers are bred to trot rather than gallop, but some reach speeds equivalent to those of galloping racehorses. Some harness racers move their legs in diagonal pairs, like riding horses, while others pace by moving their legs in lateral pairs.

Pacers race by moving lateral legs together. The left front and hind legs move at the same time, followed by the right pair of legs.

Goggles protect a jockey's eyes from flying turf and dirt.

The groom shifts her weight to help steer the carriage around the obstacles.

Contestants aim to complete the course without knocking down the balls or the cones.

Scurry driving

Scurry driving combines speed with accuracy. Drivers and ponies race around a twisting course of up to 20 pairs of bollards or cones, each pair set just wide enough apart for the wheels of the carriage to pass through. Driving trials is another popular driving sport. Similar to ridden horse trials, competitors take part in three phases: dressage, the marathon, and an obstacle course.

TEAM SPORTS

TEAM SPORTS are fast and demand special skills from horse and rider. Polo is one of the oldest and most popular of sports, while polocrosse and horseball have been introduced more recently. To take part in team sports, horses and riders must be fit. Riders need quick reactions and good balance for making fast, sharp turns. Team sports are played on ponies and small horses.

Le Trec

Le Trec began in France about 25 years ago, and is divided into three phases. The first is orienteering, in which riders follow a map at set speeds. The second judges the control of a horse's paces. The third involves jumping, cross-country, and dismounted exercises.

The net is used to scoop and throw a soft, rubber ball.

Polo

Each team has four players whose aim is to score by hitting the ball into the opposing team's goal. Player number one attacks, number four defends, while the other two mark the centre. A match consists of four to six "chukkas", each lasting seven minutes.

The attacking player must score as many goals as possible.

Riders can hook an opponent's stick.

Polocrosse

Polocrosse teams consist of six players. Each team is divided into two so that only three players from each are allowed on the pitch at a time. Player number one is the attacker and the only one who can score a goal. Player number two takes the centre position, and player number three is the defender. A match is made up of six timed sections called "chukkas", each lasting between six and eight minutes.

Horseball

Horseball is a relatively new sport that is like basketball on horseback. Two teams of six riders aim to gain possession of a small ball with several handles. Four from each team are allowed on the pitch at a time, and the ball must be kept in the air. Riders try to take the ball from the opposing team, and then score a goal.

Horseball is played in many countries, and is particularly popular in France.

Riders are allowed to "ride off" by bumping into an opponent and pushing them off line.

Polo ponies are, in fact, horses that stand between 15 hh and 15.2 hh.

Players must always hold the polo stick in their right hand.

39

HOMEWARD BOUND

WHEN YOU HAVE finished competing, tend to your horse. Before heading for home cool down your horse and check for minor injuries and loose shoes. Wash any mud from its legs to uncover hidden cuts and remove shoe studs if used. Allow your horse to drink, but make sure the water is not too cold. Once back at home, make sure your horse is comfortable before finishing for the day.

Care of grass-kept horse

At the show, cool down a grass-kept horse as you would any other horse. At home, check that the horse is comfortable; it should not be shivering and the base of its ears should feel warm. If necessary, stable and rug up the horse until it is dry and comfortable enough to turn out. Otherwise, turn it out so that it can walk around and roll.

Rolling helps dry off a sweaty coat and relaxes the horse.

Cooling down

Before going home, make sure your horse has cooled down, so that it doesn't get a chill. Walk the horse round, with a rug on if necessary; it may not need a rug in hot weather. If it is hot and humid, alternate walking your horse with washing it down until the horse is comfortable.

Muscle cramp may occur if you leave your horse standing still immediately after working hard. Walk it quietly to allow it to relax, and make sure its temperature is stable.

Unload with care. A tired horse may trip or stumble.

Coming home

Put a rug on your horse to travel home. A light rug or summer sheet is necessary even in warm weather to prevent tired muscles cramping up and as protection from draughts in a moving vehicle. Offer the horse a drink before you leave the show and give it a haynet to help it relax during the journey.

In the stable

Check that your horse has travelled well and there is no sign of injury, sweating, or heat or swelling in the legs. If you are worried, get expert advice; check the horse's legs first thing the next morning. Put on stable rugs, then make sure the horse has hay and water and a clean, deep bed. If the horse is dry and relaxed, feed as normal. Before finishing for the day, check over the horse, and add or change rugs if necessary.

Give the same quantity and type of feed as normal. Clean water must be available.

41

SAFETY AT A SHOW

COMPETING puts extra demands on you and your horse, so it is important to make sure you both stay safe. Use the right clothes and equipment and make sure you only take part in well-organized competitions. A veterinary surgeon and qualified first aid experts should always be available in case of an emergency.

Special grease is smeared on the horse's legs to help it slide over cross-country fences.

Studs come in different shapes and sizes.

Brushing boots help prevent injury if the horse knocks its legs together while jumping.

Over-reach boots protect the horse's heels.

Cross-country overgirth fastens over saddle.

Rider safety

Always ride with a hat or helmet that meets the highest safety standards. It must fit properly and the harness must always be fastened. If you are jumping, especially cross-country, wear a body protector; this helps prevent injury if you fall. Replace damaged safety equipment and do not buy these items secondhand.

Horse safety

You need to protect your horse when galloping or jumping. Boots are especially important and help prevent leg injuries. They must be the right size and fastened so that they do not slip, but are not too tight. Studs that screw into the shoes give better grip on the ground.

Wear long-sleeved shirts to prevent your arms being scraped if you fall or ride under branches.

Wear gloves to give grip on slippery reins and check that the harness on the hat is fastened securely.

Body protectors have special panels designed to absorb impact if you fall.

Correct riding boots help you keep your feet safely in the stirrup irons.

First-aid for rider

All shows should have qualified medical help available. When you arrive at a show, find out where the first-aid base is, in case you need help. If an accident occurs try not to move an injured rider or remove the person's hat, as this may make back or neck injuries worse. Call the first-aiders or paramedics, who will know what to do. Always try to keep calm.

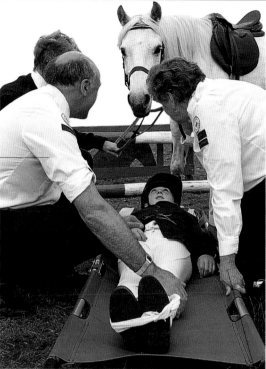

Red Cross volunteers throughout the world are trained to deal with accidents.

Veterinary on call

International competitions have veterinary surgeons in attendance. Organizers of small shows will arrange for a vet to be on call; this means that if a horse is injured, the vet can be contacted and should be there within a short time. Always take a first-aid kit so that you can deal with minor cuts and grazes.

Always call out the show vet for sudden and severe lameness.

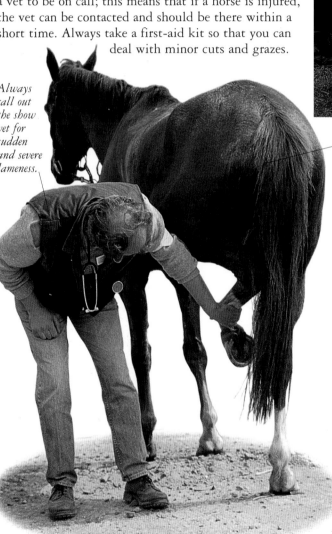

Your horse must be protected against tetanus in case of a serious cut or injury.

Trained first-aiders will know how to prepare an injured rider for safe transport to hospital.

SAFETY CHECKLIST

- When you get to the show, find the first-aid base

- Always make sure your hat harness is fastened before you get on a horse

- Keep protective boots clean and in good repair. Dirty boots may cause skin problems

- Boots cannot be worn for showing or dressage, but you can use them when warming up

- Use studs for competition only, not when riding on the road

Major Events

![ribbon icon] IF YOU REALLY ENJOY competing, and want to watch the professionals, try to take time to go shows that take place near your home.

This chart lists some of the big equestrian events that you can go to throughout the year, such as showjumping and three-day eventing.

JANUARY	FEBRUARY	MARCH
Taupo Horse Trials, NZ – Three-day event	Florida Classic, Florida, USA – Showjumping	
World Cup Showjumping, Sydney, Aus – Showjumping		
World Cup Dressage, Victoria, Aus – Dressage		
Tote Warwick Handicap Chase, Warwick, UK – Steeplechase		
The Warwick Handicap Chase is a long distance race over three miles, used by trainers as trials for the Grand National in April.		

JULY	AUGUST	SEPTEMBER
Royal International Horse Show, Hickstead, UK – Showing, showjumping, and dressage	British Jumping Derby, Hickstead, UK – Showjumping	Burghley Horse Trials, UK – Three-day event
The Tevis Cup, Auburn, USA – Endurance Ride	Goondinwindi Horse Trials, Aus – Three-day event	Royal Melbourne Show, Victoria, Au – A variety of equestrian events
	Royal Dublin Horse Show, Ireland – Showjumping	Blenheim Palace Horse Trials, UK – Three-day event
	North American Young Riders Championship, Wadworth, USA – Dressage, showjumping, and combined training	Doncaster Races, Doncaster, UK – Steeplechase
		The Little Brown Jug, Delaware, US – Pacing race
	The Hickstead Jumping Derby attracts top level riders from around the world. They come to take on the challenge of the renowned bank and Devil's Dyke obstacles.	Burghley Horse Trials is a major event in the three-day event calenda European championships are also sometimes held here.

Winners, whether of a large international event or a small local show, may receive a trophy, and some may even win money.

Riders at top international events and at local shows should always wear clothes that are clean and neat. This helps to add to the overall presentation of horse and rider in the ring.

APRIL	MAY	JUNE
Kurrajong Endurance Ride, Kurrajong, Aus – Endurance Riding	Windsor Driving Championship, Windsor, UK – Driving Trials	Royal Ascot, Ascot, UK – Flat racing
The Grand National, Aintree, UK – Steeplechase	Goodwood Dressage, Goodwood, UK – Dressage	Golden Horseshoe Ride, Exmoor, UK – Endurance riding
Rolex Kentucky Three-Day Event, Louisville, USA – Three-day event	Newmarket Races, Newmarket, UK – Flat racing	British Derby, Epsom, UK – Flat racing
Maryland Hunt Cup, Glyndon, USA – Steeplechase	Badminton Horse Trials, Gloucestershire, UK – Three-day event	Addington Dressage, Addington, UK – Dressage
	Kentucky Derby, Kentucky, USA – Flat racing	US Equestrian Team Festival of Champions, Gladstone, USA – Dressage, showjumping, and driving
The Grand National is the largest race in the racing calendar. It is run over 7 km (4.5 miles) over 30 fences.	The Badminton Horse trials were first staged in 1949 on the Duke of Beaufort's estate. It quickly became the world's leading three-day event.	The Golden Horseshoe ride is a famous British endurance event. The 160-km (100-mile) course runs over two days across the moors of Exmoor.

OCTOBER	NOVEMBER	DECEMBER
Wembley Horse of the Year Show, London, UK – Showing	Christchurch Hunter Trials, Christchurch, NZ – Three-day event	Olympia Horseshow, London UK – Showjumping
Prix de l'Arc de Triomphe, France – Flat Racing	Breeders' Cup Day, Louisville, USA – Flat racing	New Zealand Derby, Auckland, NZ – Flat Racing
Open Horseball Championship, UK – Horseball		
US Open Polo Championship, US – Polo		
The Horse of the Year Show is where horses and ponies that have won shows throughout the year meet at a grand finale.		

GLOSSARY

THERE ARE MANY WORDS associated with horses. Some have been used in this book and can be found, with a description of their meaning, below.

AIDS Signals from bodyweight, legs, voice, and hands that rider uses to communicate with horse. Whips, spurs, and martingales are considered artificial aids.

BENDING RACE Mounted game in which pony and rider gallop through a row of upright poles.

BODY PROTECTOR Protective garment for rider, designed to reduce the risk of injury in a fall.

BOUNCE FENCES Two fences set at a distance that requires a horse to jump the first, land, then jump the second without a stride in between.

BREASTPLATE Item of tack to help prevent saddle slipping back. Often used for cross-country.

BRUSHING BOOTS Prevent injury if horse strikes one leg with opposite leg or hoof.

CLEAR ROUND JUMPING Jumping competition for novice horses or riders where the aim is to jump a clear round over a low course.

COLLECTED PACE A horse is "collected" when it is perfectly balanced and its energy is gathered into short, energetic strides.

COLLECTING RING Area at a show where competitors check in before their class. Maybe used as area to warm up before entering the ring.

CREW Back-up team for endurance rider. It meets the horse and rider at stages along the ride to provide food, water, and any help.

DOUBLE FENCE Two fences in a row with one or two strides between them; distances must be correct for size of horse.

DRESSAGE Training; dressage tests are series of movements to show balance, obedience, and athletic ability of horse, and the partnership between horse and rider.

ENDURANCE RIDING Sport which involves riding long distances over set course. Distances range from 40–160 km (25–100 miles).

EVENTING Competition with three phases: dressage, cross-country, and showjumping. Also known as horse trials.

EXTENDED PACES This mean the horse's steps have controlled energy and are as long as possible.

FILLERS Brightly coloured, solid inserts in show-jumps.

FLAT RACING Races without jumps for two and three-year-old Thoroughbred horses.

GRIDWORK Gymnastic jumping exercises; jumps are set at specific distances to improve horse's athletic skill and confidence, and rider's technique.

GYMKHANA Also known as mounted games; requires an athletic pony and rider.

HARNESS RACING Driving races between horses harnessed to light two-wheeled vehicles called sulkies.

HORSE BALL Sport between two teams; each tries to get possession of a ball with handles to score a goal.

JOCKEY A rider who races horses.

LATERAL WORK Dressage and schooling exercises in which horse moves forwards and sideways at the same time.

LENGTHENED STRIDES The first stage in teaching a horse to extend its paces is to ask for strides that are longer but not faster.

OVER-REACH BOOTS Protective boots to help prevent injury if a horse strikes the heel of a front foot with the toe of a back one.

PLEASURE RIDES Non-competitive rides over distances usually between 16–32 km (10–20 miles).

POLO Fast team sport divided into intervals called chukkas; riders hit polo ball with a stick called a mallet to score goals.

POLOCROSSE Team sport which is a cross between polo and lacrosse. Riders scoop up ball with net on the end of a long handle.

QUARTER MARKS Designs made with a brush on a show horse's quarters.

REFUSAL When a horse refuses to jump or runs out to the side of a fence.

REIN BACK Dressage and schooling exercise in which horse steps backwards. The legs move in diagonal pairs.

SERPENTINE Dressage and schooling exercise in which the aim is to ride loops of equal size and shape – usually three – across the arena.

SHOWING Classes to show horse's conformation, movement, and manners. Can be ridden or in-hand.

SLOSHING DOWN Technique used to cool down endurance horses. Cold water is poured over the neck, often while horse is on the move.

STEEPLECHASING Races for Thoroughbred horses over brush fences and ditches.

TENT PEGGING Military sport; rider carries 3-m (10-ft) lance and, at a gallop, has to spear and lift peg stuck in the ground.

TREKKING Long, non-competitive pleasure rides.

VAULTING Jumping on to a moving pony without putting feet in the stirrups. An essential skill for mounted games.

VETGATE Compulsory halt during a competitive endurance ride where vet checks horse's soundness, pulse, and respiration.

INDEX

JUMPING PRACTICE

ACKNOWLEDGMENTS

Dorling Kindersley would like to thank the following people for their help in the production of this book.

The author
Carolyn Henderson has lived and worked with horses for many years. She is a regular contributor to specialist magazines such as *Horse and Hound*, and has written and edited a variety of books on all aspects of keeping, riding, and training horses.

The publishers would also like to thank the following: Hilary Bird for the index, Cheryl Telfer for additional design, and Martin Redfern for editorial assistance.

CAM Equestrian Ltd, Eardisley, Hereford for providing images of jumping poles. Lethers, Merstham, Surrey for the loan of equipment and tack. The show organizers and competitors at Chelsham Riding Club Horse Show, Farleigh, Surrey. Jackki Garnham and staff, Beechwood Riding School, Woldingham, Surrey;

Sandra Waylett, Gatton Park Livery, Reigate, Surrey; Ebbisham Farm Livery Stables, Walton on the Hill, Surrey, for use of their facilities. The models Holly Clarke, Rosie Eustace, Emma de la Mothe, Kerry Meade, and Alison Forrest. Also thanks to the horses and ponies used in photography and their owners for loaning them. These are: *Cinnamon Dust* (owned by Holly Clarke); *Eliza Doolittle* and *Ginger Pick* (owned by Sandra Waylett); *Tikki, Garochead April*, and *Meliton Bay* (owned by Jakki Garnham).

Every effort has been made to adhere to latest safety standards in the making of this book.

Picture Credits
The publishers would like to thank the following people for their kind permission to reproduce their photographs.

key: *b* bottom, *c* centre, *l* left, *t* top, *r* right

Richard Connor/Glen Tanar Equestrian Centre: 38*t*; **John**
Henderson**: 43*t*; **Kit Houghton**: 6-7; 18*b*; 21*b*; 32; 33*b*; 35*b*; 36*t*; 39*t*, *b*; 43*b*; 44*b*; **Bob Langrish**: 2; 8-9; 20*b*; 21*t*; 26*b*; 27*b*; 30*b*; 22*t*; 23*t*; 31; 33*t*; 34*t*, *b*; 35*tl*; 36*b*; 37*t*, *b*; 38*b*; 44*c*; 45*b*; 38-39.

Additional photography
Other photography was taken by **Tim Ridley**: 5*t*, 11*c*, 13; **Bob Langrish**: 11*t*, *c*, *b*; 12*t*;

Useful addresses
Here are the addresses of some societies and other organizations that you may like to contact.

British Dressage
The British Equestrian Centre
Stoneleigh, Kenilworth
Warwickshire, CV8 2LR
Tel: 01203 698837

British Horse Society, The
Stoneleigh Deer Park
Kenilworth
Warwickshire CV8 2XZ
Tel: 01926 707700

British Horse Trials Association
The British Equestrian Centre
Stoneleigh, Kenilworth
Warwickshire CV8 2LR
Tel: 01203 698856

British Show Jumping Assc
The British Equestrian Centre
Stoneleigh, Kenilworth
Warwickshire, CV8 2LR
Tel: 01203 698800

British Show Pony Society
124 Green End Road
Saltry, Huntingdon
Cambridgeshire PE17 5XA
Tel: 01487 831376

Endurance Riding Group
The British Equestrian Centre
Stoneleigh, Kenilworth
Warwickshire CV8 2LR
Tel: 01203 698863

Pony Club, The
Stoneleigh Deer Park
Kenilworth
Warwickshire CV8 2XZ
Tel: 01926 707700

Equestrian Federation of Australia
196 Greenhill Road, Eastwood
SA 5063, Australia
Tel: (08) 8357 0077

Pony Club Association of NSW
PO Box 980, Glebe
NSW 2037, Australia
Tel: (02) 9552 2800